Table Of Contents

1.
2.
3.
4.
5.
6.
7.
8.

9.
10.
11.
12.
13.
14.
15.
16.
17.
18.
19.
20.
21.
22.
23.
24.
25.
26.

Title Page

The Story of Time

As it is

A journey through the most complex, absolute, and eternal knowledge about the cycles of Time,

From the beginning till the end of creation...

Prateek Gupta

QwertyThoughts.com

Dedication

To

My loving wife, who is my life and exploration partner.

Above all, this book is dedicated to the unceasingly awake seeker in you.

About the Author

Prateek Gupta is the author of the #1 Amazon bestseller book 'Future of Time: Future That Was Written In The Past: As Per Indian Sages And Scriptures'. By profession, he is a Software Engineer and CTO of an online book publishing company QwertyThoughts.com. He is also an avid reader and began his journey of exploring history, spirituality, and the relation between them 15 years back.

"If you know the past, you can easily predict the future. And if you can predict the future, your every little action would have Integrity." And Integrity is the only thing missing from the lives of people. This is also the cause of every problem present in today's world. His aim is to bring it back into people's lives.

He can be contacted at:

kaalchakraofficial@gmail.com

linkedin.com/in/prateekgpt

fb.com/QuestionTheObviousPg

Copyright

Cover Design by Jasleen Khurana

Publisher: QwertyThoughts.com

Preface

This is how a conversation goes on when you (a Seeker) ask anything about Time to Modern day Scientists:

Seeker: Can you describe - What is a Second or a Millisecond?

Scientist - Time taken for 9,192,631,770 reverberation of cesium - 133 atom is a Second.

Seeker: But What is a Second? Are you sure the time taken for doing all the reverberation by this atom will be the same every time and everywhere in the universe?

Scientist: No Answer

Seeker: Then what is Time? If you are basing your calculations on certain movements, will it not change in different environments? Why so many 'fancy terms' created when even this is not clear?

Scientist: No Answer

Seeker: What do you think of the Vedic Time System?

Scientist: Those are just fancy terms without any scientific basis.

Seeker: Ohh, yes. Correct!

Modern science is based on the understanding of the smallest particle that they know: Quarks, which is smaller than 43 billion billionths of a centimeter (0.43 x 10−16 cm). That is astonishingly small, but what beyond that. Is there nothing smaller than Quark? Using our normal sense perceptions, there is always a difference between perception and reality. Vedic systems arose from the understanding of that absolute reality. So, the time system explained in the Vedic system is far more complex, detailed and goes beyond our knowledge of the Quark particle.

This book covers the details of the time system followed, stories, and science mentioned in scriptures in the Vedic lore. This book has also tried to include the thoughts and opinions of western scholars and scientists who have studied this system at some point in their life.

Introduction

In Indian culture, time is known as Kaala. Kaala also means death. Time is even personified as the god of death, Yam because death acts as a limiting factor in human life. Kaala determines how long a person should live on earth. So, death and time are always associated together. An individual's time on earth begins with his birth and ends with his death. However, for the soul, there is no death. It is not tied to the cycles of time and is without a beginning and without an end.

The time system followed by people living in the land of Hindus can be broadly referred to as the Vedic Time System. Kaala (Time) is regarded as a non-linear movement, like an arrow speeding from past to future. The concept of Kaala (Time) has been a very advanced idea in Hindu Heritage. It talks about rhythmic or universal order which is ultimately manifested as Time. The rhythm of Time ranges from the fast ticking of the atom to the expansion of the entire cosmos, time unfolding within the geological process of the Earth, the change of seasons, the life cycle of insects and small organisms, etc.

Kaala (Time) itself is connected to Lord Shiva in the Indian Heritage. Shiva is also called Maha Kaala — “The Lord of Time” or "The Ultimate Destroyer". His wife Kaali personifies the energy of Time.

The concept of time in Hindu culture is based came from the understanding of our own experience of how time is a recurring and predictable phenomenon that can be measured in terms of days, nights, months and years. Just as there is regularity in our days and nights, there is regularity in the days and nights of gods which is also perceived as the Rta (Rita) or the cosmic rhythm of God. Rta is inherent in every aspect of creation. In the human body, it is the biorhythm as well as the beating of the heart and the breath of the lungs. This underlying law which creates rhythms and cycles is also known as Dharma or the eternal law.

Time in the Western world is considered to be linear and is measured in the order of seconds, minutes, hours, days, weeks, fortnights, months, years, decades, and centuries. Though scientists divide seconds into milli, micro, or nanoseconds, the nomenclature still assumes a second as the basic unit. People in ancient India may not be aware of the theory of relativity but definitely familiar with the concept of space and relative time. They believed that the duration of time changed from world to world and that our time was not absolute. Here, it was successfully distinguished that there a difference between the cosmic time in other dimensions and the earthly time in which we humans live.

Here, the gods were immortal and were subject to a different time frame and had different periods of sleep, activity and rest. This made their days and nights. When the gods were awake, he would expand outwardly and manifest his objective worlds, and when it was time for rest, he would bring the worlds and the entire creation to a halt, and this all is cyclic. Modern theories of the origin of the universe also express similar theories of expansion and contraction of the our universe.

Nature of Time

Is Time Real Or Illusory?

In Hinduism, time is not viewed as a separate entity but part of the story and an important element in creation itself. It is there only until we are bound to this material aspect of this world that can be perceived only through our senses. Time is a concept created by the movement of our senses, the celestial objects around us and how we perceive them. It is a part of the illusion in which we live and take as real. There are no divisions of time. There is only a moment that is here right now every moment, which is continuous and indivisible.

As per the Shaivism stream, time is also regarded as one of the 36 tattvas or principles of creation and an important aspect of Prakriti (Nature). Prakriti subjects the boundless individual souls of pure consciousness to the limitations of time (kaala), space (niyati), knowledge (vidya), passion (raga) and power (Shakti) and binds them to the cycle of births and rebirths. When human beings transcend these five limitations, they regain pure consciousness (chit) and become free of material cycles. The Hindus view time as responsible for the absence of accurate historical records of the Indian subcontinent. The ancient Indians knew that the world is illusory, so the idea of recording events of this world didn't arise. Besides, they believed the events by themselves were of no significance unless they had some relevance to the gods and the precepts of Dharma.

Is Time Linear or Cyclic?

If we keenly observe all-natural phenomena around us, it is evident to conclude that time is repetitive, cyclic, periodic. The most evident ones are the solar cycle, rotation of the earth on its own axis and the revolution of the earth around the sun.

A seed growing into a sapling, and then to a plant eventually growing to a tree is another cyclic process that we can observe. Every seed in itself is a subtle form or blueprint of the fully grown future tree having complete genetical information of the tree. Similarly, we can observe, the sun's heat causes water to evaporate which forms clouds. Those clouds shed their water over land forming streams and rivers. Those rivers again find their way back to the ocean. And this cycle goes on forever.

Because of the way our brain functions, it ignores everything repetitive after some time. We have become so much accustomed to these phenomena, that we sometimes ignore to see these repetitive cycles. Other than these cycles, the least understood are the Human and Time cycles. To understand the complexity of human cycles with clarity, it is required to first understand that our human body is a constantly changing one, while the soul is eternal. The soul enters into a body just before birth and plays all characters like a baby, infant, child, adolescent, adult, and an elderly person and then leaves the body to take birth in another body. Again this all goes in cycles forever, until it attains Mukti (liberation).

Time neither has a beginning nor an end. So it is always represented on paper as a circle.

Every second repeats itself every 60 SECONDS. (60 seconds = 1 minute).

Every minute repeats itself every 60 MINUTES. (60 minutes = 1 hour).

Every hour repeats itself every 24 HOURS. (24 hours = 1 day).

Every day repeats itself every 365 DAYS. (365 days = 1 year).

Every year repeats itself in: ? ? YEARS

So, by that logic, every year will be repeated after a certain period of time. Can any human being be able to answer this question? Or, Can Modern Science explain this? Certainly not.

Clocks are round, the days of the week rotate, the months rotate, the seasons rotate, the yugs rotate, the mahayugs rotate, the manvantaras rotate, kalpas rotate, the planets, by which we measure time, rotate. They all indicate that time goes on round and round in cycles.

The entire existence is cyclic.

The moon revolves around Earth. Earth revolves around Sun. Sun orbits around the milky way. The Milky way revolves around another cluster of stars. That cluster revolves around a still bigger cluster. Like this how many? Beyond human imagination.

Suppose, suddenly all the objects stop revolving and become static. Then, time stops. No day or night. No winter, no summer, etc. That means the movement of astronomical bodies is the cause of time.

Can you see any linear movement in this cosmos? No. Then, how can time be linear?

Sunrises, sunsets, what happens after that? Spring, summer, autumn, winter, what comes after that?

After 12 midnight what happens? Sunset is followed by sunrise, again. After 12 midnight we get 1:00 again.

The Earth goes round and round, around the sun. Winter is followed by spring again, comes around. After December comes January, again.

This rule is followed by each object in this universe.

It's a cycle.

Time just appears to be linear. If you are familiar with Einstein's theory of relativity, it has curvature depending on the speed of our traveling and gravity at that point.

Kaalachakra

Our Universe is perishable. It originates and perishes cyclically and repeatedly. Even the creator of the universe, Brahma has birth and death. The duration between the birth and death of a Brahma is named "Mahakalpa". And the flood that comes when Brahmā dies is known as "Mahapralaya". One day of Brahma is called Kalpa kaala. In the Puraṇs, one Kalpa or one day of Brahmā is divided into 14 parts. The master of each of these divisions is called a Manu. There are fourteen Manus. The life span of every Manu is named "Manvantaram". There are 71 Chaturyugas in each Manvantara. The four yugas namely Kṛtayuga, Tretayuga, Dvaparayuga and Kaliyuga make up one Chaturyuga.

At the end of 71 such Chaturyugas, that is, at the end of every 284 (71 x 4) yugas, a Manu completes his life span. The Devas (demigods) who were born at the time of the birth of that Manu, also perishes at the end of manvantara. Fourteen such Manvantaras make one day of Brahma. Once the day of Brahma is over, the original universe perishes. Brahma's lifespan is 120 years. At the end of that period, that Brahma perishes. That is to say, at the end of every 42,200 divine days (120 x 360) which is the life span of a Brahma, a deluge takes place. Thus, in one Brahma's time, 42,200 Kalpas take place. A Brahma's life span is known as "Mahakalpa" and the close of a Brahma's period is called "Mahapralaya". And this cycle goes on.

Chronology is not Kāalagṇanām

The Hindu Kāalagṇanā (chronology) does not depend on any mundane event like the birth of a person, coronation of a king, or the military success of an emperor or army or some dynasty ruled for a specific time, a man ran away from a city to another to save his life. Instead, it depends on the movements of various cosmic bodies and astronomical science which makes Indian chronology a very scientific one.

Chronology is very subjective, as it depends on people, place or events. Kaalagnanam is the chronology of events happening since uncountable beginnings and endings of the universe.

But during the British colonial rule, the foreign rulers could have been successful to inculcate the idea that the entire concept of Hindu chronology is merely mythological fiction without having any scientific basis. As a matter of fact, those foreign rulers framed the education system of Bharatvarsh (the Indian subcontinent) with the sinister view of turning the people away from their own heritage and culture and making them respectful to whatever is Western.

The most unfortunate aspect about this is: practically nothing has been done to counter this trend during the past 73 years after gaining independence. As a result, most Indians do not even know how rich and ancient their own culture is. But on the contrary, people have developed a mentality to insult whatever is Indian. As a burning example of this trend, we are blindly following the most unscientific Christian chronology which has been thoroughly dejected and disapproved by modern science, and do not even care to know what the Indian chronology is.

Stories in Scriptures

Story 1

In an episode in the Vishnu Puran, a story goes like this that one day Vishnu, accompanied by sage Narad stops at one point in the course of their wanderings, and asks Narad to get some water for him from a nearby village. While he waits at the edge of the forest, Narad goes to the village, knocks at the door of a house. Narad falls in love with the young lady who opens the door. He marries her, starts a family, and lives happily with his wife and children for years until a flood comes and deluges the village, sweeping everything away. Narad too is washed away by the current and it happened that he was thrown exactly at the same point where he had parted company with Vishnu. When Narad lands there again, he is greeted by Vishnu who asks him, if he has found the water or not.

The pace at which TIME had moved on for Vishnu and Narad was very different.

Story 2

In Balagopalastuti of Lilashuka, there is a famous verse in which Yashoda, Krishna's mother, recites the story of Ramayan to young Krishna while she puts him to bed. The narrative reaches the point where the demon Marich, assuming the guise of a golden deer, lures Ram away from his forest hut in the hermitage, leaving Sita exposed to danger. As Yashoda was telling about the Ravan's arrival to abduct Sita, the young Krishna, being in half-sleep shouts aloud: "Lakshman! Where, Oh where, is my bow?" It was as if his past life memory of incarnation as Ram overtakes at that moment in his present life.

Suddenly Time moves in a loop.

Story 3

Another story in the Brahmavaivarta Purana speaks of the shattering of Indra's arrogance. As the king of the gods sits majestically in his palace, self-satisfied and aware of his own importance, a troop of ants moves into this assembly which takes everyone by surprise. Only one man in the assembly, seeing this strange vision, laughs aloud. When Indra asked about the reason for his laughter, he replied: each of these ants was incarnated as an Indra in one of their previous birth.

Countless cycles of Time are hinted at.

Story 4

When Narad visits Krishna's kingdom at Dwaraka, as narrated in the Bhagavat Puran, he enters the inner apartments. When he approached the senior-most queen of Krishna, he finds her attending upon Krishna with chowri (fly-whisk) in her hand. Greeting both, rishi Narad withdraws and moves towards the next chamber to pay his respects to the wife of Krishna next in seniority. And, as he enters, he sees her playing a game of dice with Krishna. In another palace he sees Krishna lying on a bed and one of his's queen massaging her soles. Amazed with what he was experiencing, he moves further and finds out that, in each chamber, a queen in Krishna's company, serving him food, helping him with oblations, and so on. In chamber after chamber, Narad encounters Krishna and is greeted by him each time as if he had seen the sage just then.

The presence of the same person at different places at a given point of time is being spoken of.

Story 5

In a story in Bhagavat Puran, again, Akrura, the great devotee of Krishna, is described as being entrusted with the responsibility of escorting Krishna and Balaram to Mathura. On his way, while going along the banks of the Yamuna river, Akrura feels the need to take a bath in the river and get refreshes. He took the permission of Krishna and Balram, stops his chariot to take a dip in the water. As he dips his head in the water, he sees Krishna and Balaram seated in the chariot below the surface of the water exactly as he had left them on the river bank. Having greatly confused, he took his head out of the water and sees both of them again on the bank in the very same chariot. Disbelieving in his senses, he takes another dip. This time, he sees Krishna as Vishnu lying on the serpent couch of Sesha in their true forms. Akrura suddenly realizes the real identity of Krishna as Vishnu, Balaram as Sesha. But when he lifts his head again out of the water, he sees Krishna and Balaram again as youthful boys engaged in conversation on the river bank.

With this sense of wonder, the elusiveness of time and appearances is depicted.

Tales like these represent the many aspects and hues of time, can be multiplied. What we understand from these is time is always moving in a cyclic fashion, making bends and loops, turning back upon itself, rising spiral-like, splitting itself, assuming different pace for different people – volatile, illusive, elusive.

Divisions of Cosmic Time

According to Surya Siddhanta, Time has both its virtual and practical divisions; the former is called murta (embodied), the latter amurta (virtual or unembodied). The Surya Siddhanta describes that, "what begins with prana (respiration) is called real; that what begins with truti is called unreal".

Vedic astronomy gives very detailed divisions of the Time up to the lowest subdivision level of Alpakāla.

Alpakāla

Alpakāla.—A short time. (Alpa=short and Kāla=time). In the Bhāgavata the following definition is given of alpakāla: "Take two tender leaves of a lotus and place one on the other. Let a strong man take a sharp needle and thrust it hard at the leaves. The time taken for the needle to pierce one leaf and reach the other is alpakāla".

Paramanu

1 Paramanu is equivalent to 60,750th of a second.

Anu

2 Paramanu = 1 Anu which is equivalent to 0.000063 seconds

Trasarenu

3 Anu = 1 Trasarenu which is equivalent to 0.00019 seconds

Truti

Thirty such alpakālas make one "Truṭi". Truti is also a Sanskrit word for a unit of measurement of weight, according to the Rasa-darpaṇa (Sanskrit work on rasaśāstra, or Medical Alchemy). Six Aṇus constitute one truṭi. It is also a period of 18 twinklings of the eye. This is also equal to approx 29.6296 microseconds or 33,750th part of the second. Truti is referred to as a quarter of the time of falling of an eyelid.

Kala

30 Truṭis = 1 Kalā.

Reṇu

60 Truṭis = 1 Reṇu, — 54,000th part of a second.

Lava

60 Reṇu = 1 Lava, — 900th part of a second.

Līkṣaka

60 Lavas = 1 Līkṣaka. — one 15th of a second.

Tatpara

1 Tatpara = 2.96296 milliseconds

Nimesha

1 Nimesha = 88.889 milliseconds

Kāṣṭhā

30 Kalās = 1 Kāṣṭhā. Time equal to 15 Nimeṣhas or 1.6 seconds, which is also known as "Nimiṣa" "Noṭi" or "Mātrā".

Gaṇita

4 Nimeshas = 1 Gaṇita

Neṭuvīrppu

10 Gaṇitas = 1 Neṭuvīrppu

Vināzhikā

6 Neṭuvīrppus = 1 Vināzhikā

Lipta

64.8 Līkṣaka = 1 Lipta

Vipala

64.8 Līkṣaka = 1 Vipala

Prāṇa

60 Līkṣakas = 1 Prāṇa, 45 nimesha = 1 Prāṇa. Equivalent to 4 seconds. 6 prāṇa = 24 seconds. It should be mentioned here that, 1 unit of prāṇa is the time an average healthy man needs to complete one respiration or to pronounce ten long syllables called guravakşara.

Pala, Vighaṭi, Vinādī

60 lipta = 1 Pala, Vighaṭi, Vinādī

Nadī

60 Vinādīs = 1 Nādi or daṇda. It is equivalent to 24 minutes.

Ahorātra

60 Nādīs = 1 Ahorātra

Vighaṭi

6 Prāṇa = 1 Vighaṭi. It is equivalent to 24 seconds.

Ghaṭi

60 Vighaṭis = 1 Ghaṭi. It is equivalent to 24 minutes.

Ghatika

30 Kala (minutes) = 1 Ghatika. It is equivalent to 24 minutes.

Kshana / Muhūrta

2 Ghatika (half hour) = 1 Kshana / Muhūrta. It is equivalent to 48 min.

The earth rotates around its axis at a speed of nearly 1660 Km per hour and its illuminated half is called ahh (day) and the dark half is called rātri (night). From the system of units of time given above, we can find that 60 Ghaţis or Nādīs make 1 day and night which is equal to 24 hours of the Western system, and a combination of this 1 human day or 1 Ahoratra. 15 such Ahoratras make 1 Paksha.

Hora

If we remove the first letter 'a' and the trailing 'tra' from 'Ahorātra' that we have seen in the last chapter, one is left with the word horā, and from this horā, another system of measuring time, the 'Horā System', was introduced in this country by the celebrated Hindu astronomer Varāha Mihira, by dividing a day and night into 24 horās.

It is from this Horā System, the entire world has adopted the present practice of dividing a day and night into 24 hours. Etymologically the word hour is derived from Anglo-Norman houre, which is derived from Old French houre which again derived from Latin hōra which is taken from Sanskrit horā,

It is interesting to note here that, we can derive the names of the seven days of a week from Horā System as well.

Nakṣhatra Māsam

2 Pakshas and 30 Stellar days = 1 Nakṣhatra Māsam or Chandra Masam (lunar month). Equivalent to 1 Month.

Nakshatras or Daily Stars

The Ancient Hindu Sages divided the 360 degrees of the elliptic sky around us into 27 Nakshatras or lunar constellations or simply sectors. Each constellation covers 13 degrees, 20 minutes. The moon travels through one Nakshatra in a day.

As per Hindu Puranic stories, there are 27 stars or nakshatras who are the daughters of either Daksha or Kashyapa, but wives of Chandra, the moon god. The moon god spends each night with one particular star, with whom it appears in the sky.

During its monthly cycle, the moon passes through each division roughly, once per day. According to another tradition, 27 nakshatras are associated with the nine planets or navagrahas of our solar system, with each planetary deity ruling over three particular stars. During the 27 days lunar cycle, the planetary gods enter into their respective star mansions and spend nine days with each of their three stars. The names of all 27 stars along with the planets that control them are mentioned below.

1. Ashvinī - Ketu
2. Bharanī - Shukra (Venus)
3. Krittikā - Ravi (Sun)
4. Rohini - Chandra (Moon)
5. Mrigashīrsha - Mangal (Mars)
6. Ārdrā - Rahu
7. Punarvasu - Guru (Jupiter)
8. Pushya - Shani (Saturn)

9. Āshleshā - Budh (Mercury)

10. Maghā - Ketu (south lunar node)

11. Pūrva or Pūrva Phalgunī - Shukra (Venus)

12. Uttara or Uttara Phalgunī - Surya (Sun)

13. Hasta - Chandra (Moon)

14. Chitrā - Mangala (Mars

15. Svātī - Rahu

16. Vishākhā - Guru (Jupiter)

17. Anurādhā - Shani (Saturn)

18. Jyeshtha - Budh (Mercury)

19. Mūla - Ketu

20. Pūrva Ashādhā - Shukra (Venus)

21. Uttara Ashādhā - Surya (Sun)

22. Shravana - Chandra (Moon)

23. Dhanishta - Mangala (Mars)

24. Shatabhishā - Rahu

25. Pūrva Bhādrapadā - Guru (Jupiter)

26. Uttara Bhādrapadā - Shani (Saturn)

27. Revatī - Budh (Mercury)

The calculation of Nakshatras begins with Ashwini Nakshatra: 0 degrees of Aries and ends on 30 degrees of Pisces covered by Revati Nakshatra. Abhijit is 28th Nakshatra. The use of Nakshatra is very important as per Vedic astrology. Each Nakshatra is again divided into four sections called Padas. Nakshatras also define the characteristics and qualities of the planets residing there. Knowing Janma Nakshatra is very important as per Vedic astrology. Janma Nakshatra is the Nakshatra in which the Moon was placed at the time of birth.

Seven Days of Week

Have you ever questioned that why are there seven days in a week? And from where, these seven days got their name? Well, this is also a gift from Indians to the world.

While the days seem to be arbitrarily set, but they are indeed not so. What do you think was the first thing that was visible to man? That is not too hard to answer. Of course, it is the Sun. It was the foremost and the brightest star visible in the sky. That is why it is also known as Aditya meaning 'bright'. After Sun, the next brightest body we can see in the sky is the moon which gets its light from the sun.

Apart from Sun and moon, the other brightest objects in the sky that are visible as morning and evening stars are Venus, followed by Mercury, Mars, Jupiter, and Saturn. Other than brightness, the amount of impact these 7 bodies create on earth is the reason behind these planets beings used in calculations of Indian Astrology and Astronomy. Apart from these 7, Rahu and Ketu are 2 other bodies that lie 180 degrees opposite to each other. The ascending node where the orbits of the sun and moon intersect is called Ketu, and the descending node of this intersection is named Rahu.

Instead of Sunday as per Gregorian Calendar, Saturday was the first day of the week according to the Indian system. Let's look at the revolution of each planet with respect to the earth.

Sun - 1 year

Moon - 27 days

Mercury - 87.97 days

Venus - 224.7 days

Mars - 1.88 years

Jupiter - 11.86 years

Saturn - 29.46 years

As Rahu and Ketu were intersection points of orbits, they are not taken into consideration. Keeping the time taken to finish the orbit, let's arrange them in descending order from slowest to fastest revolution. This brings us to the following:

Saturn, Jupiter, Mercury, Sun, Venus, Mars, Moon, Rahu and Ketu

If we assign these planets in the above order to each hora in a day, then planets sitting in the first hora will be the name of the day, or the planet ruling the first hora (Dinesh or Vaaresh) is the name of the day.

Earlier, we have also seen that 60 Ghaţis or Daņdas make one day and night or Ahorātra. Indian astronomy dedicated each ghaţi of the day to a planet as its lord and derived the name of the day as per the lord of the first ghaţi of the day.

Aryabhatta explained the ordering of the weekdays and their association with various grahas in Aryabhatiya, KalaKriya Pada, Verse, 16:

सप्तैते होरेशाः शनैश्चराद्या यथाक्रमं शीघ्राः|

शीघ्रक्रमाच्चतुर्था भवन्ति सूर्योदयाद् दनिपाः ||

The 7 Grahas beginning with Saturn, which is arranged in the order of increasing velocity, are the lords of the successive hours. The Grahas occurring fourth in the order of increasing velocity are the lords of the successive days, which are reckoned from Sunrise (in Sri Lanka).

Thus, this makes the lord of 24 hours as Saturn, Jupiter, Mars, Sun, Venus, Mercury, Moon counting till 24, and the fourth successive planet that occurs after calculating each lord for a day is the lord of the next day.

A similar view is mentioned in Surya Siddhanta in this Shloka.

मन्दादधः क्रमेण स्युश्चतुर्था दविसाधपिः

होरेशा सूर्यतनयादधोधः क्रमशस्तथा

Starting from Saturn downward, the Graha falling fourth is the lord of the day, downward to Saturn immediately is the lord of the hour.

Fortnight, Month and Year

Units of time bigger than days and weeks are fortnight and month. The Ṛigveda says, "aruṇo māsakṛvikah'' and Āchārya Yāska in his commentary over the verse says.

"aruṇo arocano māsakṛṇmāsānām cārddhamāsānām ca kartā bhavati"

... or the moon is the creator of months and fortnights.

In Sanskrit, the moon is called Chandrama and the lunar month is called Chandramas. During the Vedic period, people counted months and fortnights according to the phases of the moon. It was quite natural since one has to ascertain the duration of a solar month by tedious calculations, while lunar months are visible to the naked eye and therefore it is clear that solar months came into being afterward.

Fortnight can be equated with the word Pakshas in the Hindu time system. There are two types of Pakshas: Shukla and Krishna both denoting a phase of the radiance of the moon as we see from earth.

There are 12 lunar months in the Vedic calendar. These months tightly correspond to the Rashi or sector that they are orbiting, which tells us the importance and impact of the months. Below are the list of months and their corresponding ruling rashis.

1. Chaitra - Mesha

2. Vaishakha - Vrishabha

3. Jyeshtha - Mithuna

4. Ashadha - Karka

5. Sravana - Simha

6. Bhadra - Kanya

7. Ashvin - Tula

8. Kartik - Vrshchika

9. Agrahyana - Dhanush

10. Paushta - Makara

11. Magha - Magha

12. Phalguna - Meena

Hindu Seasons

These months also correspond to a specific season or change that they bring in the atmosphere around us. See how:

Vasant: Spring.

Grishma: Summer.

Varsha: Monsoon.

Sharad: Autumn.

Hemant: Pre-winter.

Shishir or Shita Ritu: Winter.

Vasant Ritu: Spring

Spring-time, or Vasant Ritu, is considered as the king of seasons for its mild, pleasant weather across India. Months of Chaitra and Vaishakh fall during this season. During this time, some important festivals, including Vasant Panchami, Gudi Padwa, Ugadi, Holi, Rama Navami, Vishu, Bihu, Baisakhi, Puthandu, and Hanuman Jayanti are celebrated.

The equinox, which marks the beginning of spring in India and the rest of the Northern Hemisphere and autumn in the Southern Hemisphere, occurs at the midpoint of Vasant. In Vedic astrology, the vernal equinox is called Vasant Vishuva or Vasant Sampat.

Grishma Ritu: Summer

Summer, which is also known as Grishma Ritu, is when the weather grows gradually hotter across most parts of India. Months of Jyeshtha and Aashaadha fall during this season. During this time, festivals like Rath Yatra and Guru Purnima are celebrated. Grishma Ritu ends on the solstice, known as Dakshinayana. It also marks the beginning of summer in the Northern Hemisphere and is the longest day of the year in India. In the Southern Hemisphere, the solstice marks the start of winter and is the shortest day of the year.

Varsha Ritu: Monsoon

The monsoon season or Varsha Ritu is the time of year when it rains heavily across much of India. Months of Shravan and Bhadrapada, or Sawan and Bhado, fall during this season. During this time, important festivals like Raksha Bandhan, Krishna Janmashtami, and Onam are celebrated throughout India. The solstice, called Dakshinayana, marks the beginning of Varsha Ritu and the official start of summer in India and the rest of the Northern Hemisphere. However, Southern India is close to the equator, so "summertime" lasts much of the year.

Sharad Ritu: Autumn

Autumn is called Sharad Ritu when the hot weather recedes gradually in most parts of India. Months of Ashwin and Kartik fall during this season. During this time, important festivals like Navaratri, Vijayadashami, and Sharad Purnima are celebrated in India. The autumnal equinox marks the beginning of fall in the Northern Hemisphere and spring in the Southern Hemisphere occurs during the midpoint of Sharad Ritu. On this date, the day and night last exactly the same amount of time. In Vedic astrology, the autumnal equinox is also known as Sharad Vishuva or Sharad Sampat.

Hemant Ritu: Pre winter

The time before winter is called Hemant Ritu. Months of Agrahayan and Paush, or Agahan and Poos, fall during this season. During this time, some of the most important Hindu festivals including Diwali, the festival of lights, Bhai Dooj, are celebrated. Hemant Ritu ends on the solstice, which marks the beginning of winter in India and the rest of the Northern Hemisphere. It is the shortest day of the year. In Vedic astrology, this solstice is known as Uttarayana.

Shishir Ritu: Winter

The coldest months of the year occur in winter, which is known as Shita Ritu or Shishir Ritu. Months of Magh and Phalgun fall during this season. During this time, important harvest festivals like Lohri, Pongal, Makar Sankranti, and the Hindu festival of Shivratri are celebrated. Shishir Ritu starts with the solstice, called Uttarayana in Vedic astrology. In the Northern Hemisphere, which includes India, the solstice signals the beginning of winter. In the Southern Hemisphere, it is the start of summer.

Samvatsar — The Year Cycles

Samvatsar is a Sanskrit term for "year". In Hindu tradition, there are 60 Samvatsars, each of which has a name. It roughly means a period of one full year sidereal when the Sun enters the sign of Aries. Some astrologers define it as the time in which Brihaspati (planet Jupiter) with its average speed crosses the journey of one zodiac sign and moves on to the next. According to this definition, when Jupiter completes the entire circle of traversing all 12 zodiac signs, it comprises 12 Samvatsars. During the entire journey, Jupiter is either close by or far from planet Earth based on which it creates positive or negative influences for an individual.

Once all 60 samvatsars are over, the cycle starts over again.

The sixty Samvatsars (Prabhava to Kshaya) are divided into three groups of 20 Samvatsars each wherein the first group of 20 Samvatsars (Prabhava to Vyaya) is assigned to Brahma, the next group of 20 Samvatsars (Sarvajit to Parabhava) to Vishnu, and the last 20 (Plavanga to Kshaya) to Shiva.

The 60 Samvatsars are:

1. Prabhava

2. Vibhava

3. Shukla

4. Pramoda

5. Prajāpati

6. Āngirasa

7. Shrīmukha

8. Bhāva

9. Yuvan

10. Dhātri

11. Īshvara

12. Bahudhānya

13. Pramāthin

14. Vikrama

15. Vrisha

16. Chitrabhānu

17. Svabhānu

18. Tārana

19. Pārthiva

20. Vyaya

21. Sarvajit

22. Sarvadhārin

23. Virodhin

24. Vikrita

25. Khara

26. Nandana

27. Vijaya

28. Jaya

29. Manmatha

30. Durmukha

31. Hemalambin

32. Vilambin

33. Vikārin

34. Shārvari

35. Plava

36. Shubhakrit

37. Shobhana

38. Krodhin

39. Vishvāvasu

40. Parābhava

41. Plavanga

42. Kīlaka

43. Saumya

44. Sādhārana

45. Virodhikrit

46. Paritāpin

47. Pramādin

48. Ānanda

49. Rākshasa

50. Anala

51. Pingala

52. Kālayukti

53. Siddhārthin

54. Raudra

55. Durmati

56. Dundubhi

57. Rudhirodgārin

58. Raktāksha

59. Krodhana

60. Kshaya

Every samvatsar has its own nature and qualities. Once the 60 names are finished, the next year starts with the first name again. This goes on in a cyclic manner.

Yug

The units of time larger than a year are called yugs. The word Yug has been derived from yoga which is derived from samyoga, or conjunction of heavenly bodies. So one finds the origin of every unit of yug to specific conjunction of the heavenly bodies in the sky.

In Indian astronomy, a yug of 5 year period to a vast Mahāyug of 4,320,000 years, are covered. Every 5 years, a conjunction of the sun and the moon occurs at the asterism Dhaniṣthā in the zodiac sign Makar (Capricorn). The sun enters Makar, in the month of Māgha. Hence the conjunction recurs every 5 years on the new-moon day in the month of Māgha and that is the basis of counting a 5-year yug.

The planet Vṛhaspati (Jupiter) takes 1 year to cover a zodiac sign and hence takes 12 years to complete its journey through all the 12 signs of the zodiac. This is the basis for counting a 12-year yug and since it originates from the motion of Vṛhaspati, it is often called the Vrāhaspatya-yug. It would be relevant to mention here that the Kumbha-Mela is held when Vṛhaspati enters the house of Kumbha (Aquarius) and hence the festival recurs every 12 years.

From the facts narrated above, one observes that a conjunction of the sun and the moon at Dhaniṣthā, while the Vṛhaspati (Jupiter) at Makar (Capricorn), occurs every 60 years and that is the basis for counting a 60-year yug. Hindu scriptures provide separate names for all the sixty years of a 60-year yug. The rare occasion when the sun, the moon and Vṛhaspati (Jupiter) meet at dhaniṣthā repeats at an interval of 865 million years. Such conjunction occurs five times in a Kalpa.

Mahayug (Chaturyug)

Beyond this level, there are 4 epochs or yugs, namely, Krita Yug, Treta Yug, Dvapara Yug, and Kali Yug. All these four yugs together are called a Chatur yug, which means "four epochs" or also termed Maha yug that means "great epochs". Together a chatur yug constitutes 4,320,000 human years and the lengths of each chatur yuga follow a ratio of (4:3:2:1:).

Yug	**Human years**	**Ratio**
krita-yug	1,728,000 years	4
treta-yug	1,296,000 years	3
dvapar-yug	864,000 years	2
kali-yug	432,000 years	1

1 Chatur yug (mahayug)= 4,320,000 human years

The ages see a gradual decline of dharma, wisdom, knowledge, intellectual capability, life span and emotional and physical strength. The amount of three gunas in the matter changes in each Yug, defining the nature of that Yug.

In the Vishnu Puran, time measurement section of the Book I - Chapter III explains the above as follows:

* 2 Ayanas (six month periods, see above) = 1 human year or 1 day of the devas

* 4,000 + 400 + 400 = 4,800 divine years (= 1,728,000 human years) = 1 Krita Yug

* 3,000 + 300 + 300 = 3,600 divine years (= 1,296,000 human years) = 1 Tretá Yug

* 2,000 + 200 + 200 = 2,400 divine years (= 864,000 human years) = 1 Dwápara Yug

* 1,000 + 100 + 100 = 1,200 divine years (= 432,000 human years) = 1 Kali Yug

* 12,000 divine year = 4 Yugs (= 4,320,000 human years) = 1 Mahayug (also called divine yug)

Manvantara

Manvantara or the age of a Manu, the progenitor of humanity, is an astronomical period of time measurement. Manvantara is a Sanskrit word, a compound word of manu and antara, manu-antara or manvantara, literally meaning the duration of a Manu or his life span. Each Manvantara is created and ruled by a specific Manu. Manu creates the world, and all its species during that period of time, upon whose death, Brahma creates another Manu to continue the cycle of Creation. Vishnu on his part takes a new Avatar, and also a new Indra and Saptarishis are appointed.

Fourteen Manus and their respective Manvantaras make one Kalpa or a 'Day of Brahma', according to the Vedic Time Cycle. At the end of each Kalpa, there is a period as long as a Kalpa of dissolution or Pralaya, wherein the worlds are destroyed and then it lies in a state of rest, which is called the 'Night of Brahma'. After the end of that night, Brahma starts his cycle of creation, throughout his life span which is 100 Brahma Varshas.

The seven Rishis, Indra, Manu, the king and his sons, are created and perished in one interval equal to seventy-one times the number of years contained in the four Yugs, with some additional years: this is the duration of the Manu, and the rest, which is equal to 852,000 divine years, or to 306,720,000 years of mortals, independent of the additional period. Fourteen times this period constitutes a day of Brahmá; the term (Bráhma) being the derivative form. The Brahma's life span is 100 Brahma varshas. The 14 Manvantaras of the current Shveta Varaha Kalpa are described below. Almost all literature refers to the first 9 Manus with the same names but there is a lot of disagreement on names after that, although all of them agree with a total of 14. We live in the 7th Manvantara. First 6 have gone, 7 more will come. In particular, their names are:

01. Svayambhuva — Son of the self-born (Beginning of creation)

Svayumbhuva Manvantara is the first phase of evolution. This manvantara started after a long night of 4320 million years when there was neither Heaven nor Earth and neither day nor night. There was nothing, but void everywhere. Then something happened and the wheel of creation started resulting in a self-generating activity. Therefore, the name of this phase was given, as Svayumbhuva, which literally means self-born.

In this Manvantara, the Saptarishis were Marichi, Atri, Angiras, Pulaha, Kratu, Pulastya, and Vashishtha. In Svayambhuva-manvantara, Vishnu's avatar was called Yajna.

02. Svarochisa — Son of the Self-Shining

The second Manvantara is Svarochisa (Svaa-ro-Chisa). The word "Svarochisa" literally means "of or pertaining to self-shining". We know that Sun is self-shining. In this phase, the creation started taking a visible form, thus, became a self-shining object at this stage which was to develop later into the golden-yellow Sun which we see today.

The Saptarishis were Urjastambha, Agni, Prana, Danti, Rishabha, Nischara, and Charvarivan. In Svarochisa-manvantara, Vishnu's avatar was called Vibhu.

03. Uttama — Son of the Most High

In the third Manvantara, this self-shining object, i.e., the Sun achieved the optimum size and the temperature to be able to maintain its family of planets. This was apparently the best stage of development and chief purpose of its formation from the living creatures' point of view. Therefore, the authors of manvantara story gave to this phase the most appropriate name of Uttama, meaning the "chief, the highest, the best", since it was during this manvantara that the Sun became a full-fledged Star.

The Saptarishis for this Manvantara were Kaukundihi, Kurundi, Dalaya, Sankha, Pravahita, Mita, and Sammita. In Uttama-manvantara, Vishnu's avatar was called Satyasena.

04. Taamasa — Son of Darkness

Taamasa (Taa-mas) is the next Manvantara. The word tamasa means "of darkness". This is the phase when for the first time the phenomenon of darkness began on Earth. And with reference to Earth, the occurrence of day and night began. The Earth got solidified and lost its earlier self-shining quality. It started throwing shadows, the era of eclipses began and when the earth-surface also remained dark because of a constant rain of meteorites lasting for millions of years.

The Saptarishis for this Manvantara were Jyotirdhama, Prithu, Kavya, Chaitra, Agni, Vanaka, and Pivara. In Taamasa-manvantara, Vishnu's avatar was called Hari.

05. Raivata — Son of wealth

In the next stage, the Earth witnessed heavy and constant rainfall lasting for millions of years, and the sky always remained overcast with clouds. rivers, lakes, oceans, mountains and landmasses were formed. Whirlwinds and whirl-pools started emerging. Movement and jumping activity began on Earth for the first time. This phase is named "Raivata manvantara" because the world "raivata" definitely signifies movement, jumping, clouds, whirlpools, rivers and mountains.

The Saptarishis for this Manvantara were Hirannyaroma, Vedasrí, Urddhabahu, Vedabahu, Sudhaman, Parjanya, and Mahámuni. In Raivata-manvantara, Vishnu's avatar was called Vaikuntha, not to be confused with Vishnu's divine realm, of the same name.

06. Chakshusha — Son of the vision

In the next Manvantara, observable life in abundance emerged everywhere. This was a natural sequence to the formation of oceans and the phenomenon of rainfall repeating on Earth more or less after definite intervals. This phase could best be explained with reference to "eyes" since all living animals and birds have eyes. Chakshu is a Sanskrit word for an eye and chakshusha (chaak-shusha) is that which is "pertaining to an eye". Hence the title chakshusha was best suited for this manvantara.

The Saptarishis for this Manvantara were Sumedhas, Virajas, Havishmat, Uttama, Madhu, Abhinâman, and Sahishnnu. In Chakshusha-manvantara, Vishnu's avatar was called Ajita.

07. Vaivasvata — Vaivasvata is the son of the Sun God (The Present Manvantara)

The seventh phase (the present one) is known as Vaivasvata Manvantara. Vaivasvata means "Vivasvat" or the Sun. In India, the Solar dynasty of kings is one of the most ancient dynasties known to history and mythology. Purans contain genealogies of kings and brahmans which start with Vaivasvata Manu. According to the story of the creation of Purans, the Vaivasvata manvantara started 120 million years ago. Hence, according to the Purans, man also emerged on Earth 120 million years ago. Although scientists' estimate of the antiquity of man goes only up to 3.75 million years, it can be shown through the proven facts of science that 120 million years of antiquity for man is not entirely impossible.

The Saptarishis for this Manvantara were Jamadagni, Kashyapa, Atri, Vashista, Gautama, Vishvamitra, and Bharadvaja. During Vaivasvata-manvantara, Vishnu's avatar is called Matsya.

The next seven stages are named Saavarnis (literally of the same color or form) with different prefixes. Saavarnis indicate the possibility of procreation of humans in the future otherwise than through the contact of male and female. Such a possibility might become a universal reality about all human beings and probably all conspicuous life only after 189 million years. Then the process of mutation of the asexual creation will be continued during the future six manvantaras. The new progeny will retain the form of its parent but the process of birth would go on changing drastically after every 309 million years.

08. Arka Saavarni (or Savarnika) — Stands with the Sun God in relationship

The Saptarishis for this Manvantara will be Diptimat, Galava, Parasurama, Kripa, Drauni (or Ashwatthama), Vyasa, and Rishyasringa. In Savarnya-manvantara, Vishnu's avatar will be called Sarvabhauma.

In the period of the eighth Manu, the name of Manu is Surya Savarnika Manu. He is the son of Surya from his second wife, Chhaya. He is thus, the half-brother to Shraddhadeva Manu. His son is Nirmoka, and among the first demigods is the Sutapas. Bali, the son of Virochana is Indra. In the age of this Manu, Vishnu's avatar will be called Sarvabhauma, the son of Devaguhya.

09. Daksha-Saavarni — Son of the Rituals

Saptarishis list: Savana, Dyutimat, Bhavya, Vasu, Medhatithi, Jyotishmán, and Satya. In Daksha-savarnya-manvantara, Vishnu's avatar will be called Rishabha.

The ninth Manu is Daksha-savarni. His son is Bhutaketu, and among the first demigods is the Marichigarbhas. Adbhuta is Indra. Rishabha would be born of Ayushman and Ambudhara.

10. Brahma-Saavarni — Son of Brahma

Saptarishis list: Havishmán, Sukriti, Satya, Apámmúrtti, Nábhága, Apratimaujas, and Satyaket. In Brahma-savarnya-manvantara, Vishnu's avatar will be called Vishvaksena.

In the period of the tenth Manu, the name of Manu is Brahma-savarni. Among his sons is Bhurishena, the demigods are the Suvasanas, and Sambhu is Indra. Vishvaksena would be a friend of Sambhu and will be born from the womb of Vishuchi in the house of a brahmana named Visvasrashta.

11. Dharma-Saavarni — Son of the Eternal Law

Saptarishis list: Niśchara, Agnitejas, Vapushmán, Vishńu, Áruni, Havishmán, and Anagha. In Dharma-savarnya-manvantara, Vishnu's avatar will be called Dharmasetu.

In the period of the eleventh Manu, the name of Manu is Dharma-savarni, who has ten sons, the eldest one being Satyadharma. Among the demigods is the Vihangamas, and Indra is known as Vaidhrita. Dharmasetu will be born of Vaidhrita and Aryaka.

12. Rudra-Saavarni — Son of the Destroyer

Saptarishis list: Tapaswí, Sutapas, Tapomúrtti, Taporati, Tapodhriti, Tapodyuti, and Tapodhan. In Rudra-savarnya-manvantara, Vishnu's avatar will be called Sudhama.

In the period of the twelfth Manu, the name of Manu is Rudra-savarni, whose eldest son is headed by Devavan. The demigods are the Haritas and others, and Indra is Ritadhama. Sudhama, or Shrvadhama, who will be born from the womb of Sunrita, wife of a Satyasaha.

13. Deva-Saavarni — Son of the Shining

Saptarishis list: Nirmoha, Tatwadersín, Nishprakampa, Nirutsuka, Dhritimat, Avyaya, and Sutapas. In Deva-Lavanya-manvantara, Vishnu's avatar will be called Yogeshwara.

In the period of the thirteenth Manu, the name of Manu is Deva-savarni. Among his sons is Chitrasena, the demigods are the Sukarmas and others, and Indra is Divaspati. Yogeshwara will be born of Devahotra and Brihati.

14. Indra-Saavarni — Son of the mighty Indra

Saptarishis list: Agnibáhu, Śuchi, Śhukra, Magadhá, Gridhra, Yukta, and Ajita. In Indra-savarnya-manvantara, Vishnu's avatar will be called Brihadbhanu.

In the period of the fourteenth Manu, the name of Manu is Indra-savarni. Among his sons are Uru and Gambhira, the demigods are the Pavitras and others, and Indra is Suchi. Brihadbhanu will be born of Satrayana from the womb of Vitana.

Kalpa — A Cosmic Day of Brahmā

Kalpa (Sanskrit: "period of time; or a cycle of time." from a verb-root klrip (to be in order) — a sequence of one thousand mahayugas is called a kalpa which is one day in the life of Brahma. The universe exists during Brahma's day and is dissolved during Brahma's night.

Sometimes a kalpa is called the period of a Mahamanvantara - or "great manvantara" - after which the globes of a planetary chain no longer go into obscuration or repose, as they periodically do, but die utterly. A kalpa is also called a Day of Brahma, and its length is 4,320,000,000 years. Seven rounds form a Day of Brahma, or a planetary manvantara.

Seven planetary manvantaras (or planetary cycles, each cycle consisting of seven rounds) form one solar kalpa (or solar manvantara), or seven Days of Brahma - a week of Brahma.

In this cyclic process of time, 1000 chaturyuga or mahayuga period is called a Kalpa, and the period of time is equal to the daytime for the Brahma, the creator of the universe. A thousand and a thousand (i.e. two thousand) chaturyugs are said to be one day and night of Brahmā (the creator).

1 kalpa = 1000 chaturyug (mahayug)

1 day and 1 night of Brahmā = 2 kalpas

At the beginning of creation begins the day of creation. At the end of that goes back all of the creation of the Absolute. This is a Kalpa a cosmic cycle of becoming and either of creation and destruction.

Mahakalpa

Brahma (the creator) lives for 100 years of 360 such days and at the end, he is said to dissolve, along with his entire Creation, into the Paramātman (Eternal Soul). The scriptures put Brahma's age at 100 years in his unique time scale.

Brahma's life span is equal to 311,040,000,000,000 human years. This period is named maha kalpa. A universe lasts only for one maha kalpa period. At the end of it, the universe is completely destroyed together with the creator Brahma and a new universe would be created with a new Brahma. This cycle goes on endlessly. The Vedic universe passes through repetitive cycles of creation and destruction. During the annihilation of the universe, energy is conserved, to manifest again in the next creation.

1 Maha Kalpa = 100 years of Brahma (311,040,000,000,000 human years).

The Cosmic Years

Time of the Devas — The Cosmic Years

1 day of the Devas is 1 human year

1 month of the Devas is 30 days of the Devas

1 year of the Devas (1 divine year) = 12 months of the Devas

The lifespan of the Devas is 100 years of the Devas i.e. 36,000 human years.

Current age of the creation

According to Surya Siddhanta, the current Kaliyug began at midnight of 18th February in 3,102 BC in Julian Calendar. In the current year of 2021, we are in the 5,123rd solar year, according to the Kaliyug calendar. At the grossest level, it is believed that the current Brahma is in his 51st year of age. Considering that his one day and night is equal to 2000 Mahayugas, each Mahayug comprising 4,320,000 earth years, according to popular belief, it would surely be mind-boggling to calculate how many earth years have elapsed since Brahma in the current cycle of Mahakalpa was born.

So in 14 Manvantars, the number of years

1,728,000 x 15 = 25,920,000

(Number of year in Satyug) + 14 Manvantar = 4,294,080,000

1 Kalpa = 4,320,000,000 years

One day & night of Brahma = 4,320,000 Mahayug x 100 = 4,320,00,000 years

Since the one moment in the life of Brahma is considered to be of our 100 years, therefore the life of Brahma in 100 years will be

4,320,000,000 x 360 x 100 = 1,555,200,000,000 years

The Present Age of Cosmos according to the Vedic System is as follows:

As of 2021 AD of the Roman calendar, we are on the first day after the 50th birthday of Creator Lord Brahma. On that first day, we are in the 28th Kaliyug of the 7th Manvantar. 5,123 years of Kaliyug have already elapsed and 426,877 years still remain. Putting it all together this brahmand is a little over 154 trillion human years old and will last for another 154 trillion human years. Calculating age of this creation:

1 Parardha = 154,586,880,000,000

6 Manvantars = 6 * 306,720,000 = 1,840,320,000

27 Chaturyug = 27 * 4,320,000 = 116,640,000

1 Sat + 1 Treta + 1 Dwapar = 11,664,000

5,123 years of Kaliyug = 5,123

Age of this creation = 154,588,848,629,123

Remaining Time of this creation = 154,584,911,370,877

Current Yug

Kaliyug lasts for 432,000 years and is the 4th of 4 yugs in a cycle as well as the current yug, with two sandhyas (dawn), each lasting for 36,000 years:

Kaliyug started 3,102 BCE in past:

= current year + Kaliyug start year

= 2021 + 3102

= 5,123 years

Kaliyug-sandhya (dawn) ends 32,899 CE in future:

= Kaliyug-sandhya + elapsed Kaliyug

= 36,000 - (2,021 + 3,102)

= 30,879 years

Kaliyug-sandhyamsa (dusk) starts 392,899 CE in future:

= Kaliyug - Kaliyug-sandhyamsa - elapsed Kaliyug

= 432,000 - 36,000 - (2,021 + 3,102)

= 390879 years

Kaliyug ends 428,899 CE in future:

= Kaliyug - elapsed Kaliyug

= 432,000 - (2,021 + 3,102)

= 426,879 years

Current Chatur Yug

A Chatur yug lasts for 4.32 million years, where the current is the 28th of 71 chatur yug:

Started 3,891,102 BCE in past:

= Chatur yug - Kaliyug + elapsed Kaliyug

= 4,320,000 - 432,000 + (2,021 + 3,102)

= 3,893,123 years

≈ 3.89 million years

Ends 428,899 CE in future:

= Kaliyug - elapsed Kaliyug

= 432,000 - (2,021 + 3,102 - 1)

= 426,878 years

Current Kalpa

A kalpa (day of Brahma, 12 hours) lasts for 4.32 billion years, where the current (Shveta-Varaha Kalpa) is the 1st of 30 kalpas in his 1st month of his 51st year:

Started in past:

= elapsed 7th manvantara + 7 manvantara-sandhyas + 6 manvantaras

= elapsed 28th chatur-yuga + 27 chatur-yugs + 7 manvantara-sandhyas + 6 manvantaras

= chatur-yuga - Kaliyug + elapsed Kaliyug + 27 chatur-yugs + 7 manvantara-sandhyas + 6 manvantaras

= ((4,320,000 - 432,000 + (2,021 + 3,102)) + 4,320,000 * 27) + 1,728,000 * 7 + 306,720,000 * 6

= 1,972,949,123 years

≈ 1.97 billion years

Ends in future:

= remaining 7th manvantara + 8 manvantara-sandhyas + 7 manvantaras

= remaining 28th chatur-yuga + 43 chatur-yugs + 8 manvantara-sandhyas + 7 manvantaras

= Kaliyug - elapsed Kaliyug + 43 chatur-yugs + 8 manvantara-sandhyas + 7 manvantaras

= ((432,000 - (2,021 + 3,102)) + 4,320,000 * 43) + 1,728,000 * 8 + 306,720,000 * 7

= 2,347,050,879 years

≈ 2.35 billion years

Current Maha Kalpa

A Maha Kalpa (life of Brahma) lasts for 311.04 trillion years:

Started in past:

= elapsed 18,001st kalpa + 18,000 kalpas + 18,000 pralayas

= elapsed 7th manvantara + 7 manvantara-sandhyas + 6 manvantaras + 36,000 kalpas/pralayas

= elapsed 28th chatur-yuga + 27 chatur-yugs + 7 manvantara-sandhyas + 6 manvantaras + 36,000 kalpas/pralayas

= chatur-yuga - Kaliyug + elapsed Kaliyug + 27 chatur-yugs + 7 manvantara-sandhyas + 6 manvantaras + 36,000 kalpas/pralayas

= (((4,320,000 - 432,000 + (2,021 + 3,102)) + 4,320,000 * 27) + 1,728,000 * 7 + 306,720,000 * 6) + 4,320,000,000 * 36,000

= 155,521,972,949,123 years

≈ 155.52 trillion years

Ends in future:

= remaining 18,001st kalpa + 17,999 kalpas + 18,000 pralayas

= remaining 7th manvantara + 8 manvantara-sandhyas + 7 manvantaras + 35,999 kalpas/pralayas

= remaining 28th chatur-yug + 43 chatur-yugs + 8 manvantara-sandhyas + 7 manvantaras + 35,999 kalpas/pralayas

= Kaliyug - elapsed Kaliyug + 43 chatur-yugs + 8 manvantara-sandhyas + 7 manvantaras + 35,999 kalpas/pralayas

= (((432,000 - (2,021 + 3,102)) + 4,320,000 * 43) + 1,728,000 * 8 + 306,720,000 * 7) + 4,320,000,000 * 35,999

= 155,518,027,050,879 years

≈ 155.52 trillion years

Daily Sankalp

Traditionally in Hindu Sanskriti, before performing any work we undertake Sankalp which is a declaration to ourselves and to the supreme power within us. According to Vedas, it is said that the whole Universe is evolved through a Sankalp of Lord SriManNaaraayan or Vishnu.

Sankalp is a Sanskrit word, which can be vaguely translated to 'resolution' in English; meaning free will or determination. The word Sankalp also means good intention, an oath or a resolution to do something, a sincere pledge to do something good. Sankalp also means a proposal to do something good in a Vedic or a Shastric way. In any religious ceremony or ritual generally, we observe a person taking a Sankalp (firm resolve) to achieve the purpose of the ceremony in spite of facing troubles in its achievement.

Sankalp shloka and its Significance

Sankalp is usually performed by sitting in Padmasan by clasping the right palm over the left; rested on the right thighs near the knee. After chanting the Sankalp mantra usually, some flowers and rice is taken in the right-hand palm are dropped in the Arghya patra using water. Sometimes only water is used. A Vedic Sankalp generally comprises of the elements of Time; Location; Almanac (Panchanga); Lineage; Purpose; Wish or desire; Target (the Deity); and nature or mode of karma. It starts with...

Sri Govinda Govinda! subhe sobana muhurthe; Sri MahaVishnor Aagnaaya; Pravarthamaanasya...

Time Element: (Estimating time with reference to Brahma)

Some of the terms used in Sankalp shloka containing the time element are-

Aadhya Brahmana, Dwiteeya Parardhe, Swetha Varaha Kalpe, Vaivaswatha Manwanthare, Kaliyuge, Prathama Pade, Salivahana Sakhe.

In this, there is the reckoning of the current date as per Vedas since the birth of Brahma.

Aadya Bramhane Dwiteeya Parardhe: This means the first half of the lifetime of the current Brahma is over and we are in the 2nd half called Dwiteeya Parardhe; in the 51st year of Brahma (50 years of Brahma are equal to 155.52 trillion human years).

Swetha Varaaha Kalpe: that means we are currently on the first day called Swetha Varaaha Kalpa in the 51st year of Brahma; the day (Kalpa) in which Vishnu incarnated as Varaaha (great Boar).

Vaivasvata Manvantare: that means in Swetha Varaha Kalpa (1st day of Brahma) after passing through six Manvantaras out of 14; we are currently in 7th Manvantara called Vaivasvata Manvantara. In terms of a number of years after taking into account the sandhi Kalas, we have passed through 185.2416 crores human years (4320000 x 71 x 6) + (1728,000 x 7) during the previous six Manvantaras.

Ashtavimshatitamey Kaliyuge - Kali Prathama Charane: that means in the current Manvantara (Vaivasvata) we have passed through 27 Maha Yugs out of 71; currently passing through the 28th

Maha Yug. Again in this 28th Maha Yug after passing through Krita, Treta and Dwapara Yug; we are currently in Kali Yug in its first quarter after passing through 5115 years (as of 31.03.2014). As per scripts, it is said that Kali Yug had commenced in the year 3102 BC. Counting from the beginning of Kalpa it is (185.24 + 11.67 + 0.39 + 0.005) =197.30 crores human years since commencement of creation by Brahma.

Bauddhavathare: that means in the time when Lord SriManNaaraayana (Vishnu) has taken birth as Buddha.

Saalivahan Sakhe: further counting down based on the concept of Sakha, after passing through Yudhishtir and Vikrama Sakhas, we are currently in Saalivaahan Sakha; 1936 years since its beginning in 78 AD.

Geographical Element

Jambudweepe: Out of seven Dweepas (continents) on this Earth(Bhumandala), we are in Jambu Dweep (island) surrounded by Sea (Lavana Samudra)

Meror Dakshina Bhaage (paarsve): Means, to the south of Meru Parvatha a mountain which is in the center of Jambu Dweep.

Bhaaratavarshe: There are nine Varshas in this Earth, out of which we are in Bharahavarsha which is in the southern region of Meru Parvata.

Bharathakhande: In the land ruled by King Bharat

Aasethu Himachala Paryantam (present India); Near Himalaya mountains.

Godaavari Dakshina Theere: To the south of the river Godavari (this may change depending on our location)

Mama Swagrahe (my own house) or Sobhana Gruhe (rented house): This may change depending on the place where one is performing the task.

Devata Sannidhau: In the presence of the concerned devata, arriving in my house; (depending on the place where one is performing the task this may change).

Current Day Element (Description of the day)

Asmin Vartamaanena: At the present time.

Vyavahaarike – Chandramanena: As per present calendar.

Samvatsare: There are 60 years as per Lunar Calendar which gets repeated cyclically starting from Prabhava and ending with Akshaya.

Aayane: The year is divided into two segments based on the transit of Sun into Makar Rashi called Uttarayan and Kark Rashi called Dakshinayan.

Ritau: The year is again divided into six seasons starting from Vasanta followed by Greeshma, Varsha, Sharad, Hemant and Sishir.

Maase: As per Lunar Calendar, each season or ritu comprises of two months, named after the star present on the full moon day of the month starting from Chaitra and ending with Phalgun. According to the solar calendar, it is referred to as the transit of the Sun into each Zodiac (Rashi) starting from Mesh (Aries) and ending with Meen (Pisces).

Pakshe: Each month (Maas) is again divided into two fortnights; based on the Moon's position (waxing Moon or waning Moon) called Shukla Paksha (starting from Prathama to Pournami) and Krishna or Bahula Paksha (starting from Prathama to Amavasya).

Thithau: Each Paksha comprises 15 tithis out of which 14 gets repeated in both pakshas and the 15th one will be either Pournami or Amavasya.

Vaasare: There are seven days in a week starting from Sunday which gets repeated cyclically.

Nakshatre (Constellation): There are twenty-seven (27) stars in the almanac which are placed in 12 signs (Rashi) of the zodiac. These stars cyclically get repeated starting from Ashwini and ending with Revathi.

Yoge: There are 27 yogas in the almanac starting from Vishkumbha and ending with Vaidruthi. These Yogas also get repeated cyclically.

Karane: There are eleven (11) Karanas out of which seven get repeated and four occurs on specific days viz. Shukla Prathama, (Kimsthugna), Bahula Chaturdasi (Sakuni), and Amavashya (Chatushpaath, Naagava). In practice, the names of Yoga and Karana are not spelled out. Instead, it is just mentioned as Subha Yoge, Subha Karane. On some occasions, it is mentioned as Vishnu Yoge and Vishnu Karane.

Evam guna visheshana vishitayaam – Subha thitau

Element of Lineage (Gotra).

Descriptions of Rishi lineage in which one is born are generally known from forefathers. Here one's Gotra Pravara to be spelled out.

Namadheyasya: Name by which one is called.

Purpose element: One's purpose may be different according to the desire; need; cause. It could be for one's self materialistic benefits or for family reasons or for self or for performing sacred rites or for the sake of society etc.

Reference to the specific Deity: Addressing the deity for which the specific ritual is being performed.

Reference to the name, nature and mode of ritual: The ritual could be Nitya or Naimittika Karma or any specific ritual; pooja; vrata; homa; remedy; Seva; Pitra Kaarya; Dana, etc.

This reciting Sankalp is done since the beginning of culture and dates back to tens of thousands of years. Which itself tells that Indian culture knows the importance of and intricacies of time since eternity.

As per Surya Siddhant

Most people know Ravan, from the Indian epic Ramayan. However, very little is known about his father-in-law Maya's incredible accomplishments. According to legend, the Sun god, Surya, revealed the highly specific knowledge of the cosmos to Maya, presumably to allow people of Earth to better worship him.

In another sense, it can be said that Maya was able to study the science of the planet Sun and wrote down that knowledge in his book. This series of writings is known as the Surya Siddhant and it is the oldest book of astronomy known to exist. It is startlingly accurate. It is the first-ever astronomical book that records in detail about planets, stars, their orbit, their rotation and much more in detail written over 2 million years ago.

However, the present version available is believed to be more than 2500 years old, which still makes it the oldest book on earth about Astronomy.

This book covers types of time, length of the year of gods and demons, day and night of god Brahma, the elapsed period since creation, how planets move eastwards and sidereal revolution. The length of the Earth's diameter and circumference are also given. Eclipses and the color of the eclipsed portion of the moon are mentioned.

Citation of the Surya Siddhant is also found in the works of Aryabhatta.

Utpala, a 10th-century commentator of Varahamihir, quotes six shlokas of the Surya Siddhant. The present version was modified by Bhaskaracharya during the Middle Ages.

The present Surya Siddhant may still be considered a direct descendant of the text available to Varahamihir (who lived between 505–587 CE).

The Surya Siddhant is an incredible testament to the advanced thinking of ancient Indians. In this text, one can find the roots of trigonometry as well as essential mathematical inventions such as standard notation and the decimal system. In addition, the text describes gravity over a millennium before Sir Isaac Newton developed his theory in 1687. It explains sidereal revolutions and how planets move eastward. It accurately calculates the size and position of distant planets, the length of a tropical year, and the amount of time that has passed since creation. Finally, in its discussion of how time passes at different rates under different circumstances, it contains the seeds for relativity.

The tricky part about understanding Yugs in a historical context is that time is relative. Yugs pertaining to the mechanics of the universe and affairs of the gods have a different scale than those pertaining to human history.

lokānām antakṛt kālaḥ kālo 'nyaḥ kalanātmakaḥ ।

sa dvidhā sthūlasūkṣmatvān mūrtaś cāmūrta ucyate ॥ 10 ॥

(10) Time creates, maintains and destroys everything. Infinite time has no beginning or end. We are currently aware only of finite time, which has beginnings and endings. Time has both virtual and practical divisions; one is called amurta (unreal) and the other murta (real).

prāṇādiḥ kathito mūrtas truṭyādyo 'mūrtasaṃjñakaḥ ।

ṣaḍbhiḥ prāṇair vināḍī syāt tatṣaṣṭyā nāḍikā smṛtā ॥ 11 ॥

(11) That which starts with respiration (prana) is called real; that which starts with atoms (truti) is called unreal. Six breaths make a vinadi, sixty of these a nadi;

nāḍīṣaṣṭyā tu nākṣatram ahorātraṃ prakīrtitam ।

tattriṃśatā bhaven māsaḥ sāvano 'rkodayais tathā ॥ 12 ॥

(12) And sixty nadis make a sidereal day and night. Of thirty of these sidereal days is composed a month; a civil (savana) month consists of as many sunrises;

aindavas tithibhis tadvat saṃkrāntyā saura ucyate ।

māsair dvādaśabhir varṣaṃ divyaṃ tad aha ucyate ॥ 13 ॥

(13) A lunar month, of as many lunar days (tithi); a solar (saurya) month is determined by the entrance of the sun into a sign of the zodiac : twelve months make a year. This is called a day of the gods.

surāsurāṇām anyonyam ahorātraṃ viparyayāt ।

tatṣaṣṭiḥ ṣaḍguṇā divyaṃ varṣam āsuram eva ca ॥ 14 ॥

(14) The day and night of the gods and of the demons are mutually opposed to one another. Six times sixty (360) of them are a year of the gods, and likewise of the demons.

taddvādaśasahasrāṇi caturyugam udāhṛtam ।

sūryābdasaṃkhyayā dvitrisāgarair ayutāhataiḥ ॥ 15 ॥

(15) Twelve thousand of these divine years are denominated a Quadruple Age (chaturyuga); of ten thousand times four hundred and thirty-two (4,320,000) solar years.

saṃdhyāsaṃdhyāṃśasahitaṃ vijñeyaṃ tac caturyugam ।

kṛtādīnāṃ vyavastheyaṃ dharmapādavyavasthayā ॥ 16 ॥

(16) Is composed of that Quadruple Age, with its dawn and twilight. The difference between the Golden and the other Ages, as measured by the difference in the number of the feet of Virtue in each, is as follows:

yugasya daśamo bhāgaś catustridvyekasaṃguṇaḥ ।

kramāt kṛtayugādīnāṃ ṣaṣṭhāṃśaḥ saṃdhyayoḥ svakaḥ ॥ 17 ॥

(17) The tenth part of an Age, multiplied successively by four, three, two, and one gives the length of the Golden and the other Ages, in order: the sixth part of each belongs to its dawn and twilight.

yugānāṃ saptatiḥ saikā manvantaram ihocyate ।

kṛtābdasaṃkhyās tasyānte saṃdhiḥ prokto jalaplavaḥ ॥ 18 ॥

(18) One and seventy (71) Ages are styled here a Patriarchate (manvantara); at its end is said to be a twilight which has the number of years of a Golden Age, and which is a deluge.

sasaṃdhayas te manavaḥ kalpe jñeyāś caturdaśa ।

kṛtapramāṇaḥ kalpādau saṃdhiḥ pañcadaśaḥ smṛtaḥ ॥ 19 ॥

(19) In an Æon (kalpa) are reckoned fourteen such Patriarchs (manu) with their respective twilights; at the commencement of the Æon is a fifteenth dawn, having the length of a Golden Age.

ittham yugasahasreṇa bhūtasaṃhārakārakaḥ ।

kalpo brāhmam ahaḥ proktaṃ śarvarī tasya tāvatī ॥ 20 ॥

(20) The Æon, thus composed of a thousand Ages, and which brings about the destruction of all that exists, is styled a day of Brahma; his night is of the same length.

paramāyuḥ śataṃ tasya tayāhorātrasaṃkhyayā ।

āyuṣo 'rdhamitaṃ tasya śeṣakalpo 'yam ādimaḥ ॥ 21 ॥

(21) His extreme age is a hundred, according to this valuation of a day and a night ...

From the beginning of the current day of Brahma, he spent 47,400 years setting up the creation of planets, stars, gods, demons, etc.

The Surya Siddhant also goes into a detailed discussion about cycles of time and that time flows differently in different circumstances, the roots of relativity. Here we have a perfect example of Indian philosophy's belief that science and religion are not mutually exclusive.

The astronomical time cycles contained in the text were remarkably accurate at the time.

A- The tenth part of a chaturyuga, multiplied successively by four, three, two, and one, gives the length of the krita and the other yugas: the sixth part of each belongs to its dawn and twilight.

B. One and seventy chaturyugas make a manu; at its end is a twilight which has the number of years of a kritayuga, and which is a deluge.

C. In a kalpa are reckoned fourteen manus with their respective twilights; at the commencement of the kalpa is a fifteenth dawn, having the length of a kritayuga.

D. The kalpa, thus composed of 1000 chaturyugas, and which brings about the destruction of all that exists, is a day of Brahma; his night is of the same length.

E. His extreme age is a hundred, according to this valuation of a day and a night. Half of his life is past; of the remainder, this is the first kalpa.

F. And of this Kalpa, six manus are past, with their respective twilights; and of the Manu son of Vivasvat, twenty-seven chaturyugas are passed;

G. Of the present, the twenty-eighth, chaturyuga, this kritayuga is passed.

As per Manusmriti

The book of Manusmriti or the Laws of Manu contains a number of Shlokas that describes story and knowledge of time:

नमिषा दश चाष्टौ च काष्ठा त्रशित् तु ताः कला ।

त्रशित् कला मुहूर्तः स्यादहोरात्रं तु तावतः ॥ ६४ ॥

(64) Eighteen Nimeshas (twinklings of the eye, are one kashtha), thirty kashthas one Kala, thirty Kalas one muhurta, and as many (muhurtas) one day and night.

अहोरात्रे वभिजते सूर्यो मानुषदैवकि ।

रात्रिः स्वप्नाय भूतानां चेष्टायै कर्मणामहः ॥ ६५ ॥

(65) The sun divides days and nights, both human and divine, the night (being intended) for giving rest to created beings and the day for exertion.

पित्र्ये रात्र्यहनी मासः प्रवभिागस्तु पक्षयोः ।

कर्मचेष्टास्वहः कृष्णः शुक्लः स्वप्नाय शर्वरी ॥ ६६ ॥

(66) A month is a day and night of the manes (pitra), but the division is according to fortnights. The dark (fortnight) is their day for active exertion, the bright (fortnight) their night for sleep.

दैवे रात्र्यहनी वर्षं प्रविभागस्तयोः पुनः ।

अहस्तत्रोदगयनं रात्रिः स्याद् दक्षिणायनम् ॥ ६७ ॥

(67) A year is a day and a night of the gods; their division is: the half-year during which the sun progresses to the north will be the day, that during which it goes southwards the night.

ब्राह्मस्य तु क्षपाहस्य यत् प्रमाणं समासतः ।

एकैकशो युगानां तु क्रमशस्तन्निबोधत ॥ ६८ ॥

(68) Hear now, the brief of the duration of a night and a day of Brahman and of the several ages according to their order.

चत्वार्याहुः सहस्राणि वर्षाणां तत् कृतं युगम् ।

तस्य तावत्शती सन्ध्या सन्ध्यांशश्च तथाविधः ॥ ६९ ॥

(69) They declare that the Krita age (consists of) four thousand years (of the gods); the twilight preceding it consists of as many hundred, and the twilight following it is of the same number.

इतरेषु ससन्ध्येषु ससन्ध्यांशेषु च त्रिषु ।

एकापायेन वर्तन्ते सहस्राणि शतानि च ॥ ७० ॥

(70) In the other three ages with their twilights preceding and following, the thousands and hundreds are diminished by one (in each).

यदेतत् परसिङ्ख्यातमादावेव चतुर्युगम् ।

एतद् द्वादशसाहस्रं देवानां युगमुच्यते ॥ ७१ ॥

(71) These twelve thousand (years) which thus have been just mentioned as the total of four (human) ages, are called one age of the gods.

दैवकिानां युगानां तु सहस्रं परसिङ्ख्यया ।

ब्राह्ममेकमहर्ज्ञेयं तावतीं रात्रमिव च ॥ ७२ ॥

(72) But know that the sum of one thousand ages of the gods makes one day of Brahman and that his night has the same length.

तद् वै युगसहस्रान्तं ब्राह्मं पुण्यमहर्वदिः ।

रात्रर्िच तावतीमेव तेऽहोरात्रवदिो जनाः ॥ ७३ ॥

(73) Those (only, who) know that the holy day of Brahman, indeed, ends after (the completion of) one thousand ages (of the gods) and that his night lasts as long, (are really) men acquainted with (the length of) days and nights.

यद् प्राग् द्वादशसाहस्रमुदतिं दैवकिं युगम् ।

तदेकसप्ततगिुणं मन्वन्तरमहिोच्यते ॥ ७९ ॥

(79) The before-mentioned age of the gods, (or) twelve thousand (of their years), being multiplied by seventy-one, (constitutes what) is here named the period of a Manu (Manvantara).

मन्वन्तराण्यसङ्ख्यानि सर्गः संहार एव च ।

क्रीडन्नवैतत् कुरुते परमेष्ठी पुनः पुनः ॥ ८० ॥

(80) The Manvantaras, the creation and destruction of the world are infinite; sporting, as it were, Brahman repeats this again and again.

As per Atharva Ved

The concept of Time (kaala) in Vedas is described clearly with its nature, but modern science is very far away to understand or discover it. It's hard to describe in the English language, but the closest enough definition of kaala can be: The smallest form of matter which creates movements required to start the manifestation of celestial objects.

कालो अश्वो वहति सप्तरश्मिः सहस्राक्षो अजरो भूरिरेताः ।

तमा रोहन्ति कवयो विपश्चितस्तस्य चक्रा भुवनानि विश्वा ॥१॥

Kaala or Time defined as a thousand-eyed, immortal Ashwa (horse) pulling a chariot of the Universe. It is flowing continuously with seven rays and thousands of axes. Kaala never gets tired or seems not to stop as it contains tremendous force or energy. All worlds (Bhuvanani) and the Galaxies (Vishwa) are their wheels. Only the wise people tend to ride over it.

Kaala has thousands of axes on which it keeps on rotating. It rotates on the Earth around one axis, while on the other planets the time revolves around other axes. Therefore, it is different on different, innumerable solar systems, planets and galaxies. The word 'Sahasra Aksha' depicts the multiplicity of the axes.

सप्त चक्रान् वहति काल एष सप्तास्य नाभीरमृतं न्वक्षः ।

स इमा विश्वा भुवनान्यञ्जत् कालः स ईयते प्रथमो नु देवः ॥२॥

Kaala rotates the seven wheels and has seven centers around which it moves. These centers are also called Nabhis. The Kaala is the reason behind the manifestation of all worlds and galaxies. Without it, no new star will emerge. Sage Bhrigu said about Kaala: Kaala is the first God, who really moves.'

पूर्णः कुम्भोऽधि काल आहितस्तं वै पश्यामो बहुधा नु सन्तः।

स इमा विश्वा भुवनानि प्रत्यङ्कालं तमाहुः परमे व्योमन्॥ ३॥

The Kaala or Time is like a full pot. It never empties. The Kaala was present when the worlds and the galaxies took their form. It was present when space or the sky came into being. Therefore it is said to be present in the superspace.

Nasadiya Sukta of the Rigved mentions that, before the Universe came into existence there was no space and nothing else was present then. The space present before the genesis of the Universe is named the superspace.

Sage Bhrigu tells that in that superspace, Parama Wyoma (Wyoma = space), the Kaala resides.

स एव सं भुवनान्याभरत् स एव सं भुवनानि पर्यैत्।

पिता सन्नभवत् पुत्र एषां तस्माद् वै नान्यत् परमस्ति तेजः ॥४॥

Kaala is the ultimate nourisher. It supports, holds and covers them from all sides. It is said to be the father of all those who were here and descendants of all who will come. Nothing is superior or important to Kaala.

कालोऽमूं दिवमजनयत् काल इमाः पृथिवीरुत।

काले हं भूतं भव्यं चेषतिं ह्व वतिष्ठते ॥५॥

Kaala has created this sky, space and earth. Past, Present and future are decided and caused due to it.

कालो भूतमिंसृजत काले तंपतिं सूर्य्यः ।

काले ह्व वशि्वा भूतानि काले चक्षुर्विपश्यति॥ ६॥

Kaala is the reason behind this creation. It is due to Kaala that the Sun shines in the sky. All the entities and the galaxies reside in Kaala. Our eyes can see everything around it only because of Kaala.

काले मनः काले प्राणः काले नामं समाहितम्।

कालेन सर्वा नन्दन्त्यागतेन प्रजा इमाः ॥७॥

Everything is created by the Kaala. Prana is an energy superior to life. Prana controls life according to the Adhyatma Shastra and the Upanishads. Science does not know this Prana, so we will consider Prana and life as the same entity. Life and the mind all reside in the Kaala and hence they work according to the directions of the Kaala. Due to Kaala our mind thinks and proposes to work. Life, too, behaves according to the Kaala. Life comes on the Earth when the Kaala sends it and life goes away when the Kaala decides.

काले तपः काले ज्येष्ठं काले ब्रह्मं समाहितम्।

कालो ह्व सर्वस्येश्वरो यः पतिासीत् प्रजापतेः ॥८॥

Ishwar means the ruler. Kaala is the ruler of everything. Even the Brahman is situated in the Kaala. All the animate and inanimate things are produced and their producer is called Prajapati, but the Kaala produces this Prajapati.

This may sound recursive, this is what it is. The cause or basic material for building everything is Kaala.

कालः प्रजा असृजत कालो अग्रें प्रजापतिम्।

स्वयंभूः कश्यपः कालात् तपः कालादजायत ॥१०॥

Kaala produced Prajapati, who then produced all other Praja. Kaala was born from himself. Sage Kashyap, was created by the Kaala.

Science says that the Earth came into being on its own and the same science holds that nothing happens automatically, then there must be some hidden force applied. If it is true that some force is applied, then it becomes compulsory to accept the presence of some agent, who applied the force. That force and its applicator are the Kaala, according to sage Bhrigu.

Western Thought

The way Hinduism understands time is as magnificent as grandiose as the time itself. While most cultures base their cosmologies on familiar units such as few hundreds or thousands of years, the Hindu concept of time embraces billions and trillions of years. The Purans describe time units from the minuscule AlpaKala to Mahamanvantara of 311 trillion years. Hindu sages describe time as cyclic, an endless procession of creation (Brahma), preservation (Vishnu) and dissolution (Mahesh). Scientists such as Carl Sagan have expressed amazement at the accuracy of space and time descriptions given by the ancient rishis and saints, who comprehended the secrets of the Shrishti (creation) through their awakened senses.

Time in the Indian system is conceived as a wheel turning through vast cycles of creation and destruction (pralay), known as kalpa.

Joseph Campbell

In the words of Joseph Campbell, a famous writer, American professor of literature at Sarah Lawrence College who worked in comparative mythology and comparative religion:

"The Hindus with their grandiose Kalpas and their ideas of the divine power which is beyond all human category (male or female). Not so alien to the imagery of modern science that it could not have been put to acceptable use."

Huston Cummings Smith

Huston Cummings Smith was a world-famous philosopher, writer and scholar of religious studies in the United States. Has taught at MIT and was a visiting professor at Univ. of California at Berkley.

He has written various books, "The World's Religions", "Science and Human Responsibility", and "The Religions of Man". He says:

“Philosophers tell us that the Indians were the first ones to conceive of a true infinite from which nothing is excluded. The West shied away from this notion. The West likes to form, boundaries that distinguish and demarcate. The trouble is that boundaries also imprison – they restrict and confine.”

“India saw this clearly and turned her face to that which has no boundary or whatever.” “India anchored her soul in the infinite seeing the things of the world as masks of the infinite assume – there can be no end to these masks, of course. If they express a true infinity.” And it is here that India’s mind-boggling variety links up to her infinite soul.”

“India includes so much because her soul being infinite excludes nothing.” It goes without saying that the universe that India saw emerging from the infinite was stupendous.”

While the West was still thinking, perhaps, of 6,000 years old universe – India was already envisioning ages and eons and galaxies as numerous as the sands of the Ganges. The Universe, so vast that modern astronomy slips into its folds without a ripple.”

Dr. Carl Sagan

Dr. Carl Sagan in his book Broca's Brain: Reflections on the Romance of Science, says:

“Immanuel Velikovsky, in his book Worlds in Collision, notes that the idea of four ancient ages terminated by catastrophe is common to Indian as well as to Western sacred writing.

However, in the Bhagavad Gita and in the Vedas, widely divergent numbers of such ages, including an infinity of them, are given; but, more interesting, the duration of the ages between major catastrophes is specified as billions of years...”

“The idea that scientists or theologians with our present, still puny understanding of this vast and awesome cosmos, can comprehend the origins of the universe is only a little less silly than the idea that Mesopotamian astronomers of 3,000 years ago – from whom the ancient Hebrews borrowed, during the Babylonian captivity, the cosmological accounts in the first chapter of Genesis – could have understood the origins of the universe. We simply do not know.

The Hindu holy book, the Rig Veda (X:129), has a much more realistic view of the matter:

“Who knows for certain? Who shall here declare it?

Whence was it born, whence came creation?

The gods are later than this world’s formation;

Who then can know the origins of the world?

None knows whence creation arose;

And whether he has or has not made it;

He who surveys it from the lofty skies,

Only he knows- or perhaps he knows not.”

Hinduism is the only religion that propounds the idea of the life cycles of the universe. It suggests that the universe undergoes an infinite number of deaths and rebirths. Hinduism, according to Carl Sagan, “… is the only religion in which the time scales correspond… to those of modern scientific cosmology.

Long before Aryabhata (6th century) came up with this awesome achievement, apparently there was a mythological angle to this as well — it becomes clear when one looks at the following translation of Bhagavad Gita (part VIII, lines 16 and 17),

“All the planets of the universe, from the most evolved to the most basic, are places of suffering, where birth and death takes place. But for the soul that reaches my Kingdom, O son of Kunti, there is no more reincarnation. One day of Brahma is worth a thousand of the ages known to humankind; as is each night.”

Thus each kalpa is worth one day in the life of Brahma, the God of creation. In other words, the four ages of the mahayuga must be repeated a thousand times to make a “day of Brahma”, a unit of time that is the equivalent of 4.32 billion human years, doubling which one gets 8.64 billion years for a Brahma's day and night. This was later theorized (possibly independently) by Aryabhatta in the 6th century. The cyclic nature of this analysis suggests a universe that is expanding to be followed by contraction, a cosmos without end. This, according to modern physicists is not an impossibility.

Professor Arthur Holmes

Arthur Holmes was a professor at the University of Durham and a British geologist who made two major contributions to the understanding of geology. He writes regarding the age of the earth in his great book, The Age of Earth (1913) as follows:

“Long before it became a scientific aspiration to estimate the age of the earth, many elaborate systems of the world chronology had been devised by the sages of antiquity. The most remarkable of these occult time-scales is that of the ancient Hindus, whose astonishing concept of the Earth’s duration has been traced back to Manusmriti, a sacred book.”

"The Hindu religion is the only one of the world's great faiths dedicated to the idea that the Cosmos itself undergoes an immense, indeed an infinite, number of deaths and rebirths. It is the only religion in which the time scales correspond, to those of modern scientific cosmology. Its cycles run from our ordinary day and night to a day and night of Brahma, 8.64 billion years long. Longer than the age of the Earth or the Sun and about half the time since the Big Bang. And there are much longer time scales still."

Maurice Polydore Marie Bernard Maeterlinck

Maurice Polydore Marie Bernard Maeterlinck, also known as Count Maeterlinck from 1932, was a Belgian playwright, poet, and essayist who was Flemish but wrote in French who won the 1911 Nobel Prize for literature. In his book Mountain Paths says:

“he falls back upon the earliest and greatest of Revelations, those of the Sacred Books of India with a Cosmogony which no European conception has ever surpassed.”

In Hindu thought, interspersed between linear, time-limited existences lie timeless intervals of non-existence. The creation hymn of the Hindus, Nasadiya-sukta of Rig-Veda, affirms an absolute beginning of things and describes the origin of the universe as being beyond the concepts of existence and non-existence.

“The Hindu pictured the universe as periodically expanding and contracting and gave the name Kalpa to the time span between the beginning and the end of one creation. The scale of this space or time is indeed staggering. It has taken more than two thousand years to come up again with a similar concept.”

Hindu culture had this unique vision of the infiniteness of time as well as the infinity of space. When modern astronomy deals with billion of years, Hindu creation concepts deal with trillions of years. Vedanta upholds the idea that creation is timeless, having no beginning in time. Each creation and dissolution follows in sequence. The whole cosmos exists in two states — the unmanifested or undifferentiated state and the manifested or differentiated state.

Guy Sorman

According to Guy Sorman, French-American professor, columnist, author, and public intellectual in economics and philosophy, visiting scholar at Hoover Institution at Stanford and the leader of new liberalism in France:

"Temporal notions in Europe were overturned by an India rooted in eternity. The Bible had been the yardstick for measuring time, but the infinitely vast time cycles of India suggested that the world was much older than anything the Bible spoke of. It seems as if the Indian mind was better prepared for the chronological mutations of Darwinian evolution and astrophysics."

Alan Wilson Watts

Alan Wilson Watts, a British philosopher, writer and speaker, research fellow of Harvard University, known for interpreting and popularizing Buddhism, Taoism, and Hinduism for a Western audience drew heavily on the insights of Vedanta. Watts became well known in the 1960s as a pioneer in bringing Eastern philosophy to the West. He wrote:

“To the philosophers of India, however, Relativity is no new discovery, just as the concept of light years is no matter for astonishment to people used to thinking of time in millions of kalpas (a kalpa is about 4,320,000 years). The fact that the wise men of India have not been concerned with technological applications of this knowledge arises from the circumstance that technology is but one of the innumerable ways of applying it.”

It is, indeed, a remarkable circumstance that when Western civilization discovers Relativity it applies it to the manufacture of atom-bombs, whereas Oriental civilization applies it to the development of new states of consciousness.”

Dick Teresi

Dick Teresi, author of several books about science and technology, including The God Particle has written for Discover, The New York Times Magazine, and The Atlantic Monthly. He says

"Indian cosmologists, the first to estimate the age of the earth at more than 4 billion years. They came closest to modern ideas of atomism, quantum physics, and other current theories. India developed very early, enduring atomist theories of matter. Possibly Greek atomistic thought was influenced by India, via the Persian civilization."

"The big bang is the biggest-budget universe ever, with mind-boggling numbers to dazzle us – a technique pioneered by fifth-century A.D. Indian cosmologists, the first to estimate the age of the earth at more than 4 billion years. The cycle of creation and destruction continues forever, manifested in the Hindu deity Shiva, Lord of the Dance, who holds the drum that sounds the universe's creation in his right hand and the flame that, billions of years later, will destroy the universe in his left. Meanwhile, Brahma is but one of untold numbers of other gods dreaming their own universes. The 8.64 billion years that mark a full day-and-night cycle in Brahma's life is about half the modern estimate for the age of the universe. The ancient Hindus believed that each Brahma day and each Brahma night lasted a kalpa, 4.32 billion years, with 72,000 kalpas equaling a Brahma century, 311,040 billion years in all. That the Hindus could conceive of the universe in terms of billions."

Paul Joseph Steinhardt

Paul Joseph Steinhardt, an American theoretical physicist and professor in Science at Princeton University whose principal research is in cosmology and condensed matter physics and Cambridge University's Neil Turok, have recently developed 'The Cyclical Model'.

They have just fired their latest volley at that belief, saying there could be a timeless cycle of expansion and contraction. It's an idea as old as Hinduism, updated for the 21st century. The theorists acknowledge that their cyclic concept draws upon religious and scientific ideas going back for millennia — echoing the "oscillating universe" model that was in vogue in the 1930s, as well as the Hindu belief that the universe has no beginning or end, but follows a cosmic cycle of creation and dissolution.

(source: Questioning the Big Bang - msnbcnews.com)

Sir Monier Monier-Williams

Sir Monier Monier-Williams, a professor of Sanskrit at Oxford University, England who studied, documented and taught Asian languages, especially Sanskrit, Persian and Hindustani says:

"The Hindus were Spinozists more than 2,000 years before the advent of Spinoza, and Darwinians many centuries before Darwin and Evolutionists many centuries before the doctrine of Evolution was accepted by scientists of the present age."

Louis Jacolliot

Louis Jacolliot, a French historian, barrister, colonial judge, author and lecturer. says, "Here to mock our conceit, our apprehensions, and our despair, we may read what Manu said, perhaps 10,000 years before the birth of Christ about Evolution:

'The first germ of life was developed by water and heat.' (Manusmriti - Book I, shloka 8,9)

'Water ascends towards the sky in vapors; from the sun it descends in rain, from the rains are born the plants, and from the plants, animals.' (Manusmriti - Book III, shloka 76)

Sir John Woodroffe

Sir John Woodroffe, (1865-1936) also known by his pseudonym Arthur Avalon, was a British Orientalist whose extensive and complex published works on the Tantras, and other Hindu traditions, stimulated a wide-ranging interest in Hindu philosophy and yoga. He was also an Advocate-General of Bengal and Legal Member of the Government of India. He served with competence for 18 years and in 1915 officiated as Chief Justice. He has said:

"Ages before Lamarck and Darwin it was held in India that man has passed through 84 lakhs (8,400,000) of birth as plants, animals, as an "inferior species of man" and then as the ancestor of the developed type existing today.

"The theory was not, like the modern doctrine of evolution, based wholly on observation and a scientific inquiry into a fact but was a rather (as some other matters) an act of brilliant intuition in which observation may also have had some part."

Thus, in Hinduism, science and religion are not opposed fundamentally, as they often seem to be in the West, but are seen as parts of the same great search for truth and enlightenment that inspired the sages of Hinduism. Fundamental to the Hindu concept of time and space is the notion that the external world is a product of the creative play of Maya (illusion).

"The Hindu religion is the only one of the world's great faiths dedicated to the idea that the Cosmos itself undergoes an immense, indeed an infinite, number of deaths and rebirths. It is the only religion in which the time scales correspond, to those of modern scientific cosmology.

"It is the clearest image of the activity of God which any art or religion can boast of." Modern physics has shown that the rhythm of creation and destruction is not only manifest in the turn of the seasons and in the birth and death of all living creatures, but also the very essence of inorganic matter.

For modern physicists, then, Shiva's dance is the dance of subatomic matter. Hundreds of years ago, Indian artists created visual images of dancing Shiva's in a beautiful series of bronzes. Today, physicists have used the most advanced technology to portray the pattern of the cosmic dance. Thus, the metaphor of the cosmic dance unifies, ancient religious art and modern physics.

Fritjof Capra

Fritjof Capra, Austrian-born American physicist, systems theorist, and deep ecologist wrote:

"Modern physics has thus revealed that every subatomic particle not only performs an energy dance but also is an energy dance; a pulsating process of creation and destruction. The dance of Shiva is the dancing universe, the ceaseless flow of energy going through an infinite variety of patterns that melt into one another''. For the modern physicists, then Shiva's dance is the dance of subatomic matter. As in Hindu mythology, it is a continual dance of creation and destruction involving the whole cosmos; the basis of all existence and of the all-natural phenomenon. Hundreds of years ago, Indian artists created visual images of dancing Shivas in a beautiful series of bronzes. In our times, physicists have used the most advanced technology to portray the patterns of the cosmic dance."

Nancy Wilson Ross

Nancy Wilson Ross, an American novelist. A native of Olympia, Washington who graduated from the University of Oregon in 1924, became an expert in Eastern religions and wrote fifteen novels including The World of Zen and Time's Left Corner made her first trip to Japan, China, Korea and India in 1939. She has written:

"Anachronistic as this labyrinthine mythology may appear to the foreign mind, many of India's ancient theories about the universe are startlingly modern in scope and worthy of a people who are credited with the invention of the zero, as well as algebra and its application of astronomy and geometry; a people who so carefully observed the heavens that, in the opinion of Monier-Williams, they determined the moon's synodical revolution much more correctly than the Greeks."

" Many hundreds of years before those great European pioneers, Galileo and Copernicus, had to pay heavy prices in ridicule and ex-communication for their daring theories, a section of the Vedas known as the Brahmanas contained this astounding statement:

"The sun never sets or rises. When people think the sun is setting, he only changes about after reaching the end of the day and makes night below and day to what is on the other side. Then, when people think he rises in the morning, he only shifts himself about after reaching the end of the day-night and makes day below and night to what is on the other side. In truth, he does not see at all."

"The Indians, whose theory of time, is not linear like ours – that is, not proceeding consecutively from past to present to future – have always been able to accept, seemingly without anxiety, the notion of an alternately expanding and contracting universe, an idea recently advanced by certain Western scientists. In Hindu cosmology, immutable Brahman, at fixed intervals, draws back into his beginning-less, endless Being the whole substance of the living world. There then takes place the long "sleep" of Brahman from which, in course of countless eons, there is an awakening, and another universe or "dream" emerges. "

"This notion of the sleeping and waking, or contracting and expanding, of the Life Force, so long a part of Hindu cosmology, has recently been expressed in relevant terms in an article written for a British scientific journal by Professor Fred Hoyle, Britain's foremost astronomer. "

Lord Vishnu is said to rest in the coils of Ananta, the great serpent of Infinity, while he waits for the universe to recreate itself.

“Plainly, contemporary Western science’s description of an astronomical universe of such vast magnitude that distances must be measured in terms as abstract as light-years is not new to Hinduism whose wise men, millennia ago, came up with the term kalpa to signify the inconceivable duration of the period elapsing between the beginning and end of a world system.

“It is clear that Indian religious cosmology is sharply at variance with that inherited by Western peoples from the Semites. On the highest level, when stripped of mythological embroidery, Hinduism’s conceptions of space, time and multiple universes approximate in range and abstraction the most advanced scientific thought. ”

Dr. Heinrich Zimmer

Dr. Heinrich Zimmer, a German Indologist and linguist, as well as a historian of South Asian art, a man of penetrating intellect observed:

“In one of the Puranic accounts of the deeds of Vishnu in his Boar Incarnation or Avatar, occurs a casual reference to the cyclic recurrence of the great moments of myth. The Boar, carrying on his arm the goddess Earth whom he is in the act of rescuing from the depths of the sea, passingly remarks to her:

“Every time I carry you this way….”

For the Western mind, which believes in single, epoch-making, historical events (such as, for instance, the coming of Christ) this casual comment of the ageless god has a gently minimizing, annihilating effect.”

Edward Washburn Hopkins

Edward Washburn Hopkins, an American Sanskrit scholar born in Northampton, Massachusetts received the degree of Ph.D. in 1881 became a professor of Sanskrit and comparative philology at Yale University in 1895 says:

"Plato is full of Sankhyan thought, worked out by him, but taken from Pythagoras. Before the sixth century B.C. all the religious-philosophical ideas of Pythagoras are current in India (L. Schroeder, Pythagoras). If there were but one or two of these cases, they might be set aside as accidental coincidences, but such coincidences are too numerous to be the result of the change. "

And again he writes: "Neo-Platonism and Christian Gnosticism owe much to India. The Gnostic ideas in regard to a plurality of heavens and spiritual worlds go back directly to Hindu sources. Soul and light are one in the Sankhyan system before they became so in Greece, and when they appear united in Greece it is by means of the thought which is borrowed from India. The famous three qualities of the Sankhyan reappear as the Gnostic 'three classes.'

Story of Creation and Destruction

In various purans, a story of creation and destruction of the universe is mentioned in extreme detail, but in personified form. If we consider each entity or body as a cosmic body instead of a person, the science behind it is right in front of us.

Story of Creation

Before the creation of our universe, Vishnu, the preserver lies asleep on the ocean of all causes. Vishnu is resting on a serpent bed with thousands of cobras beneath. While asleep, a lotus sprouts from his navel. From this lotus, Brahma, the creator of the universe is born. He the lives for next hundred years and dies.

One year of Brahma consists of 360 days. At the beginning of each day, Brahma creates the living creatures at the beginning of each day and is absorbed into him at the end of each day while he sleeps on a lotus. Each day of Brahma is known as a Kalpa. Within each Kalpa, there are fourteen Manus and within each Manu are 71 Chaturyugs. Each Chaturyugs is divided into four parts called Yugapadas.

Story of Destruction (Pralay)

According to the story of time (kaala), it says: "all the beings of this universe including the creator Brahma and other gods are ruled by me. They are created, preserved and are destroyed by me but I, cannot be destroyed".

The Cyclical Destruction of the World occurs in events singularly known as a Pralay that takes place at the end of a Chatur-Yug. A cycle of Four Yugs is known as a Maha Yug or a Chatur-Yug. At the end of Chatur-Yug, our Earth experiences a series of disastrous events which has the capacity to wipe out all life from the planet.

Purans describes different types of Pralayas in detail:

(1) Nitya Pralay is the sleep or by an extension thereof, Death.

(2) A Pralay at the end of a Chatur-Yug (every 4.32 Million Solar Years),

(3) Manvantar Pralay at the end of each of Manavantas (every 307 Million Solar Years),

(4) Naimittik Pralay is the end of a single day of Brahma (4.32 Billion Solar Years) when the three worlds (Bhuh: Bhuvaha: and Suvaha disintegrate,

(5) Prakritik Maha Pralay at the end of Brahma's Lifetime (311.4 Trillion Solar Years)!

Natraj - Cosmic Dance

Shiva is symbolized as an embodiment of energy. His dance is an example of that energy. 'Nataraj' literally means the King of Dance (Nritya) and there is a lot of science and physics behind Shiva's cosmic dance.

According to scientific research, the cosmic dance of Shiva (tandava) symbolizes the interaction between the static and dynamic energy flows. This energy flow contains principles of creating, destructing, preserving, creating illusions, and liberating. The unique appearance of Nataraj is enclosed in a ring of fire, represents by the cyclic and continuous creation and destruction of the universe. The three matters: space, time and mass are called to be enclosed within this Natraj's ring of fire.

On his upper right hand, he holds the Damru (small hourglass-shaped drum) which represents creation and time. His lower right hand is in Abhay Mudra or blessing pose. His upper left-hand holds fire a symbol of destruction. His lower left hand is lifted near to his chest and his palms facing down. This symbolizes mastery over meditation and enlightenment. His right leg is placed on a demon named Apasmara (a dwarf who represents spiritual ignorance and nonsensical speech), which denotes the end of ignorance. The skull which is present over his head denotes complete victory over death.

So, Shiva's cosmic dance is also known as the dance of bliss and symbolizes the rhythm of birth and death and cosmic cycles of creation and destruction. As per modern physics, Shiva's dance has been defined as a continuous dance of subatomic matter denoting the birth and death of matter.

Lord Shiva has won the name of Nataraj and there is a beautiful story about how that happened:

Once Shiva and Goddess Kali decided to see who of them both was the best in dance and expression. Vishnu became the Judge. Shiva's dance was natural and effortless. His expressions were such that they flowed along with every movement. Each demigod and sage who witnessed it was mesmerized. Goddess Kali did in the same way too, following his every pose and expression with the same grace. Then Shiva lifted his right leg, dipped it in kumkum (saffron), and touched Goddess Kali's forehead with it, applying Kumkum to her. Goddess Kali was surprised. She couldn't do that to her husband. She smiled at him and stopped her dance. That was when Lord Shiva was declared 'Nataraj' by Vishnu.

"As per the quantum theory too, the very existence of matter is based on this dance of creation and destruction. Modern physics tells us that every subatomic particle is a reverberating process of creation and destruction and also keeps performing an energy dance. For the modern physicists then, Shiva's dance is the perfect dance of subatomic matter and also the very basis of all existence and all-natural phenomena."

An American physicist Fritjof Capra expounded in his book 'The Tao of Physics' that "Experiments in Modern physics has reached to a point where it is able to find out that the cycles of creation and destruction are not only present in the turn of the seasons or in the process of birth and death of all living beings but it is also the very essence of any inorganic matter".

Capra concluded by saying that: "Thousands of years back, Indian artists created stunning artistic impressions of dancing Shiva in bronze. In our times, physicists have portrayed the patterns of cosmic dance using the most advanced technology. The metaphor of the cosmic dance of Natraj unifies modern physics, religious art, and ancient mythology."

An English writer and philosopher Aldous Huxley wrote:

"The whole thing is there itself, you experience around yourself a world of space and time, matter and energy, the world of creation and destruction, the world of psychology. West doesn't have anything which is even close to such a comprehensive story that is cosmic, psychological yet spiritual."

The most common forms of Shiva's dance are of two types: first is Lasya, which is the gentle form of dance associated with the creation of the world, and the other is Tandava, which is a violent form of dance having association with the destruction of weary worldviews, perspectives & lifestyles.

Conclusion

In this long story of the universe and understanding of time, this book is a stepping stone to explore the horizon of the phenomenon. The more we explore, the more we see is unexplored.

I am inviting you to take the next step and leap towards reality. Click on the link below or scan the QR code to join the community of similar explorers and seekers.

https://www.facebook.com/groups/781011122430423

See you on the other side,

Prateek

Printed in Great Britain
by Amazon

40842448R00057